1892

821
SM1

Scorpion

AND OTHER POEMS

By the same author

Novels

NOVEL ON YELLOW PAPER

OVER THE FRONTIER

THE HOLIDAY

Poetry

A GOOD TIME WAS HAD BY ALL

TENDER ONLY TO ONE

MOTHER, WHAT IS MAN?

HAROLD'S LEAP

NOT WAVING BUT DROWNING

SOME ARE MORE HUMAN THAN OTHERS

SELECTED POEMS

THE FROG PRINCE AND OTHER POEMS

TWO IN ONE

*   *   *

CATS IN COLOUR

Scorpion

AND OTHER POEMS
WITH DRAWINGS BY THE AUTHOR
AND AN INTRODUCTION BY
PATRIC DICKINSON

Stevie Smith

Longman

LONGMAN GROUP LIMITED
LONDON

*Associated companies, branches and
representatives throughout the world*

This edition © Stevie Smith 1972

*All rights reserved. No part of this
publication may be reproduced, stored in
a retrieval system, or transmitted in any
form or by any means, electronic,
mechanical, photocopying, recording, or
otherwise, without the prior permission
of the Copyright owner.*

First published 1972
Second impression 1972

ISBN 0 582 12708 4

PRINTED IN GREAT BRITAIN
BY W & J MACKAY LIMITED, CHATHAM

CONTENTS

ACKNOWLEDGEMENTS

Most of these poems were first published in the following newspapers and periodicals: *Ambit, The Guardian, The Listener, New Statesman, Observer, The Sunday Times* and *The Times Literary Supplement*. 'How do you see?' was commissioned by *The Guardian*, 'Cock-a-Doo' by The Camden Festival, and 'Francesca in Winter' by Poem of the Month Club.

The Poetry of Stevie Smith
by Patric Dickinson

Being unique is by no means an advantage. Nor must unique-
ness be confused with originality. Every good poet is original.
He has his own rhythm, his own 'voice'. For example Robert
Graves, developing from his Georgian beginnings, has refined
his 'originality', has tempered his style to its present spare
rhythm and power of simple diction. Reading Yeats from beginning to end one has this same particular delight in seeing this
heightening of their powers, and one might compare them to
deciduous trees. But, to continue the metaphor, they are planted
in the demesne of English poetry, in a traditional soil. How-
ever much they have enriched, modified, or changed the course
of English poetry, they remain 'as trees walking'—a mysteri-
ous but natural-seeming phenomenon.

There is, very rarely, another kind of poet who seems like
the dragon's teeth sown before the building of Thebes. These
spring up into fully-armed men, at once, by magic. So, one
might say, de la Mare sprang up fully-armed, and remained
so; so also two of the greatest original American poets, Robert
Frost and Emily Dickinson. Frost and de la Mare, in very
different ways, refined upon an original gift and both are just
within tradition, Frost transferring to New England the direct,
pastoral, and practical speech of Wordsworth; de la Mare refin-
ing upon his gift for being the Shakespeare who wrote lyrics
such as 'Full Fathom Five', and his extraordinary knowledge
of folklore, nursery-rhyme, and his natural instinct for super-
natural experience, as typified in our Ballads, which are earthy,
macabre, magical and direct. It is a complete mistake to imagine
that Walter de la Mare is soppy. His other-world creatures
are, like the fairy in *Mrs Gill*, usually malevolent; as are Stevie
Smith's.

All these very different poets have in common a real and a

fantasy world. What happens when there is no barrier between worlds? It seems to me that one gets a kind of poetical seventh child. (In the Ballads it is always the seventh child who is untrustworthy, murderous, or inexplicable, a kind of creature sprung from nowhere, as the armed men must have seemed to the oppressed Cadmus, founder of Thebes—an extra blow of fate.)

Such poets as Emily Dickinson and Stevie Smith sprang from such a nowhere. Both are unique and original; incomparable and inimitable.

In Emily Dickinson's case most of her finest, and worst, work is based on the four-line stanza of hymn tunes. This simple form, combined with her astonishingly original, unexpected and economic use of words, has now become well-enough known, and she is recognised as one of America's greatest poets. To put down what these two very different women have in common without *comparing* them is extremely difficult, for though both are unique and original, they are wholly different in their poetic outlook; their qualities are different, and I am not disposed to give them 'rankings'.

Both share a running quarrel with God, in which God could seldom get in even an edgewise word; both had a kind of direct Mayflowering approach; neither could stomach the conventional or conventicle approach. Yet the hymn tune rhythm is there always, and often, in them both, satirically. Emily immured herself, though not so harshly as is supposed; Stevie lived an open hard-working life, in a City office; and it is good to record that in the last few years she had the recognition which she had always deserved; and, I think, desired; and, I know, enjoyed.

'Whose poetry do you read, Miss Smith?' a questioner asked her once when I was with her on a tour of recitals. With a perfectly enchanting (and I mean the word in its *proper* sense) and a sly innocence; and a sidelong look at me; she answered 'Why, *nobody's* but my own.'

In the same way, Emily let down from her window home-made gingerbread in a basket to the Jenkins children from next door, often with cryptic little notes. The two poets share a penchant for a kind of conspiracy which will harm nobody and yet be potent for the truth, and the 'secret that shall never be told'.

But it is time, after saying what company she keeps, to write of Stevie Smith, alone, wandering on 'the sweet prairies of anarchy'.

This kind of prairie was her own demesne, and she planted or sowed as she chose. It is a strange place: it has frog princes; jungle-husbands who 'hitapotamus'; various eccentric and very sensible people; nearly all her people are aspects of poems, rather than vice versa. The technique she used is, apart from hymn tune, a kind of running line of natural speech, a doggerel verse, sometimes tacked together with awful deliberate rhymes, thrown at one with a devil-may-care obviousness. But these are preserved, and alive, and free from banality, because of the strength of her devil-*will*-care morality, and her sharp wit. She could not abide cruelty, either in humans towards humans, or humans towards the animal world. No-one but Stevie could have quizzed the roles of cats and dogs and pets in general (including humans) with quite such a compassionately exact eye as to name a cat Hopdance and a dog Clanworthy; names of generic genius; ark-names.

She illustrated her poems with line-drawings, which are funny; pathetic; or tender; never sentimental or cruel. James Thurber had a similar, but different gift, using much the same line. In his case, the goofy dogs and 'dreadfully ugly' humans take that order of precedence. Stevie Smith never drew caption-less cartoons; her drawings illuminate and render meaning to poems, an extra pleasure, not a necessary or explanatory comment; and the humans, dotty or not, predominate over lesser creations but, paradoxically, without any domination.

The combination of wit, tolerance, and an absolute standard of minimum and maximum in human intelligence and emotion is not common. Stevie Smith had this, by instinct and by natural genius; but also by a great deal of thought and study, both in theology and poetry. At a cursory reading she might be taken to be a kind of 'Sunday' poet. It would be difficult to find a poet more sophisticated. The technique she chose to employ is, likewise, shrewd, naïve, and devilishly clever, with a hint of God correcting the proofs; and indeed in this sense she was a 'Sunday' poet with a feeling for Sunday as opposed to other days of the week like a lapsed Catholic; but she wrote about all the other days; and her hours, days, or weeks or years are the poems she wrote. Some people have no time for them and say they are not poems. Others who have entered this curious timeless world of satire, tender or brutal fairy-tale, often sardonic moral comment, and disturbing, sometimes terrifying, insight into the lives they know they lead, and suspect their friends and enemies of leading, will mourn for the loss of this poet who

> 'Spoke no more than grace allowed
> And no less than truth,'

but they need not, save in the aspect that the unique talent cannot mortally offer more. What is there is there, in the words of another poet 'for as long as forever is'.

Scorpion

'This night shall thy soul be required of thee'
My soul is never required of *me*
It always has to be somebody else of course
Will my soul be required of me tonight perhaps?

(I often wonder what it will be like
To have one's soul required of one
But all I can think of is the Out-Patients' Department—
'Are you Mrs Briggs, dear?'
No, I am Scorpion.)

I should like my soul to be required of me, so as
To waft over grass till it comes to the blue sea
I am very fond of grass, I always have been, but there must
Be no cow, person or house to be seen.

Sea and *grass* must be quite empty
Other souls can find somewhere *else*.

O Lord God please come
And require the soul of thy Scorpion

Scorpion so wishes to be gone.

Seymour and Chantelle
or
Un peu de vice

(in memory of A. Swinburne and Mary Gordon)

PULL my arm back, Seymour,
Like the boys do,
Oh Seymour, the pain, the pain,
Still more then, do.
I am thy schoolboy friend, now I
Am not Chantelle any more but mi.
Say 'sweet mi', 'my sweet mi.' Oh the pain, the pain,
Kiss me and I will kiss you again.

Tell me, Seymour, when they . . . when . . .
Does it hurt as much as this
And this and this? Ah what pain.
When I do so I feel
How very painful it is for you,
No I will, so, again and again,
Now stuff the dockleaves in your mouth
And bite the pain.

Seymour, when you hold me so tight it hurts
I feel my ribs break and the blood spurt,
Oh what heaven, what bliss,
Will you kiss me, if I give you this
Kiss, and this and this? Like this?

Seymour, this morning Nanny swished me so hard
(Because I told her she had the face
Of an antediluvian animal that had
Become extinct because of being so wet)
She broke her hair-brush. What bliss.
No, don't stop me now with a kiss, oh God it was pain-
Ful, I could not stop crying.

Oh darling, what heaven, how did you think
Of doing that? You are my sweetest angel of a
Little cousin, and your tears
Are as nice as the sea, as icy and salt as it is.

How do you see?

How do you see the Holy Spirit of God?
I see him as the holy spirit of good,
But I do not think we should talk about spirits, I think
We should call good, good.

But it is a beautiful idea, is it not?
And productive of good?

Yes, that is the problem, it is productive of good,
As Christianity now is productive of good,
So that a person who does not believe the Christian faith
Feels he must keep silent, in case good suffers,
In case what good there is in the world diminishes.

But must we allow good to be hitched to a lie,
A beautiful cruel lie, a beautiful fairy story,
A beautiful idea, made up in a loving moment?

Yes, it is a beautiful idea, one of the most
Beautiful ideas Christianity has ever had,
This idea of the Spirit of God, the Holy Ghost,
My heart goes out to this beautiful Holy Ghost,
He is so beautifully inhuman, he is like the fresh air.
They represent him as a bird, I dislike that,
A bird is parochial to our world, rooted as we are
In pain and cruelty. Better the fresh fresh air.

But before we take a Christian idea to alter it
We should look what the idea is, we should read in their
    books
Of holy instruction what the Christians say. What do they
    say
Of the beautiful Holy Ghost? They say

4

That the beautiful Holy Ghost brooded on chaos
And chaos gave birth to form. As this we cannot know
It can only be beautiful if told as a fairy story,
Told as a fact it is harmful, for it is not a fact.

But it is a beautiful fairy story. I feel so much
The pleasure of the bird on the dark and powerful waters,
And here I like to think of him as a bird, I like to feel
The masterful bird's great pleasure in his breast
Touching the water. Like! Like! What else do they say?

Oh I know we must put away the beautiful fairy stories
And learn to be good in a dull way without enchantment,
Yes, we must. What else do they say? They say

That the beautiful Holy Spirit burning intensely,
Alight as never was anything in this world alight,
Inspired the scriptures. But they are wrong,
Often the scriptures are wrong. For I see the Pope
Has forbidden the verse in Mark ever to be discussed again
And I see a doctor of Catholic divinity saying
That some verses in the New Testament are pious forgeries
Interpolated by eager clerks avid for good.

Ah good, what is good, is it good
To leave in scripture the spurious verses and not print
A footnote to say they are spurious, an erratum slip?

And the penal sentences of Christ: He that believeth
And is baptised shall be saved, he that believeth not
Shall be damned. Depart from me ye cursed into everlasting
    fire
Prepared for the devil and his angels. And then
Saddest of all the words in scripture, the words,
They went away into everlasting punishment. Is this good?

Yes, nowadays certainly it is very necessary before we take
The ideas of Christianity, the words of our Lord,
To make them good, when often they are not very good,
To see what the ideas are and the words; to look at them.

Does the beautiful Holy Ghost endorse the doctrine of
    eternal hell?
Love cruelty, enjoin the sweet comforts of religion?
Oh yes, Christianity, yes, he must do this
For he is your God, and in your books

You say he informs, gives form, gives life, instructs.
Instructs, that is the bitterest part. For what does he instruct
As to the dreadful bargain, that God would take and offer
The death of the Son to buy our faults away,
The faults of the faulty creatures of the Trinity?
Oh Christianity, instructed by the Holy Ghost,
What do you mean? As to Christ, what do you mean?

It was a child of Europe who cried this cry,
Oh Holy Ghost what do you mean as to Christ?
I heard him cry. Ah me, the poor child,
Tearing away his heart to be good
Without enchantment. I heard him cry:

Oh Christianity, Christianity,
Why do you not answer our difficulties?
If He was God He was not like us
He could not lose.

Can Perfection be less than perfection?
Can the creator of the Devil be bested by him?
What can the temptation to possess the earth have meant
    to Him
Who made and possessed it? What do you mean?

And Sin, how could He take our sins upon Him? What does
    it mean?
To take sin upon one is not the same
As to have sin inside one and feel guilty.

It is horrible to feel guilty,
We feel guilty because we are.
Was He horrible? Did He feel guilty?

You say He was born humble—but He was not,
He was born God—

7

Taking our nature upon Him. But then you say
He was perfect Man. Do you mean
Perfectly Man, meaning wholly? Or Man without sin? Ah
Perfect Man without sin is not what we are.

Do you mean He did not know that He was God,
Did not know He was the Second Person of the Trinity?
(Oh if He knew this and was,
It was a source of strength for Him we do not have)
But this theology of emptying you preach sometimes—
That He emptied Himself of knowing He was God—seems
A theology of false appearances
To mock your facts, as He was God whether He knew it
    or not.

Oh what do you mean, what do you mean?
You never answer our difficulties.

You say, Christianity, you say
That the Trinity is unchanging from eternity,
But then you say
At the incarnation He took
Our Manhood into the Godhead
That did not have it before,
So it must have altered it,
Having it.

Oh what do you mean, what do you mean?
You never answer our questions.

So I heard the child of Europe cry,
Tearing his heart away
To be good without enchantment,
Going away bleeding.

Oh how sad it is to give up the Holy Ghost
He is so beautiful, but not when you look close,
And the consolations of religion are so beautiful,
But not when you look close.
Is it beautiful, for instance, is it productive of good
That the Roman Catholic hierarchy should be endlessly
     discussing at this moment
Their shifty theology of birth control, the Vatican
Claiming the inspiration of the Holy Spirit? No, it is
     not good,
Or productive of good. It is productive
Of contempt and disgust. Yet
On the whole Christianity I suppose is kinder than it was,
Helped to it, I fear, by the power of the Civil Arm.

Oh Christianity, Christianity,
That has grown kinder now, as in the political world
The colonial system grows kinder before it vanishes, are
     you vanishing?
Is it not time for you to vanish?

I do not think we shall be able to bear much longer the
     dishonesty
Of clinging for comfort to beliefs we do not believe in,
For comfort, and to be comfortably free of the fear
Of diminishing good, as if truth were a convenience.
I think if we do not learn quickly, and learn to teach children,
To be good without enchantment, without the help
Of beautiful painted fairy stories pretending to be true,
Then I think it will be too much for us, the dishonesty,
And, armed as we are now, we shall kill everybody,
It will be too much for us, we shall kill everybody.

The Ass

In the wood of Wallow
Mash, walked Eugenia, a callow
Girl, they said she was,
An Ass.

Beyond the wood there lay a soppy mórass
But the path across was firm, was
Not a-wash.

Three years in the wood Eugenia stayed
By briar and bramble and lost ways she was delayed,
And in a witch's house within a thicket of yew trees
Was put to work, but seemed so happy that the witch
Finding no pleasure in her tyranny
Gave her release.
She is an ass, she cried, let her pass.
And perish in the soppy mórass.

Eugenia was as happy in the change
To be free to roam and range
As she had been happy and not sad or sorry
At her labours in the witch's bothy.
The sun fell hot upon the causeway
That was not very wide
And the mórass sopped and shuffled
Either side.

And the little beetles ran
About, and all the gnats and the mosquitos sang
And the mórass was as sweet a green
As Eugenia had ever seen.

She sang: Baa-baa-ba-bay
And seven happy years spent on the way.

Once there came a fiend
Who tempted her to go upon the green
Morass: Come, ass, and go
Upon the green. But she said, No.
She was not such an ass to try the green,
It would deliver her below.

Heigh-ho, heigh-ho,
Never was such a happy idle ass
Since idleness ran glad in Paradise
As Eugenia was.
Paradise. Paradise.

Now the seven years have passed,
The causeway's ended, the soppy mórass
Has sucked its last; the ass
Comes to a sandy pass
Between low sandhills that are tufted
          over the esparto grass.
Beyond, the great seas splash
And roll in pleasure to be so a-wash,
Their white crests coming at a dash
To fetch the ass.

Oh my poor ass
To run so quickly as if coming home
To where the great waves crash.
Now she is gone. I thought
Into her tomb.

Yet often as I walk that sandy shore
And think the seas
Have long since combed her out that lies
Beneath, I hear the sweet ass singing still with joy as if
She had won some great prize, as if
All her best wish had come to pass.

A Soldier Dear to Us

I т was the War
I was a child
They came from the trenches
To our suburb mild.

Our suburb then was more a country place
They came to our house for release.

In the convalescent Army hospital
That was once a great house and landed estate
Lay Basil, wounded on the Somme,
But his pain was not now so great

That he could not be fetched in a bath-chair
Or hobble on crutches to find in our house there
My mother and aunt, his friends on leave, myself (I was
      twelve)
And a hearth rug to lie down in front of the fire on and rest
      himself.

It was a November golden and wet
As there had been little wind that year and the leaves were
      yet
Yellow on the great trees, on the oak trees and elms
Of our beautiful suburb, as it was then.

When Basil woke up he liked to talk and laugh
He was a sweet-tempered laughing man, he said:
'My dear, listen to this' then he read
From The Church Times, how angry the Bishop was because
Of the Reserved Sacrament in the church
Of St Alban's, Holborn. 'Now, my dear' he said, 'for a treat
Next Sunday I will take you to All Saints, Margaret Street;
    only
You will have to sit on the ladies' side, though you are not
    yet one really.'

Basil never spoke of the trenches, but I
Saw them always, saw the mud, heard the guns, saw the
    duckboards,
Saw the men and the horses slipping in the great mud, saw
The rain falling and never stop, saw the gaunt
Trees and the rusty frame
Of the abandoned gun carriages. Because it was the same
As the poem 'Childe Roland to the Dark Tower Came'
I was reading at school.

Basil and Tommy and Joey Porteous who came to our house
Were too brave even to ask *themselves* if there was any hope
So I laughed as they laughed, as they laughed when Basil
    said:
What will Ronny do now (it was Ronny Knox) will he pope?

And later, when he had poped, Tommy gave me his book for
    a present,
'The Spiritual Aeneid' and I read of the great torment
Ronny had had to decide, Which way, this or that?
But I thought Basil and Tommy and Joey Porteous were
    more brave than that.

Coming to our house
Were the brave ones. And I could not look at them,
For my strong feelings, except
Slantingly, from the hearth rug, look at them.

Oh Basil, Basil, you had such a merry heart
But you taught me a secret you did not perhaps mean to
    impart,
That one must speak lightly, and use fair names like the
    ladies
They used to call
The Eumenides.

Oh Basil
I was a child at school,
My school lessons coloured
My thoughts of you.

ENVOI

Tommy and Joey Porteous were killed in France. Now
    fifty years later
Basil has died of the shots he got in the shell crater
The shrapnel has worked round at last to his merry heart,
    I write this
For a memorial of the soldier dear to us he was.

The Forlorn Sea

OUR Princess married
A fairy King,
It was a sensational
Wedding.

Now they live in a palace
Of porphyry,
Far, far away,
By the fòrlorn sea.

Sometimes people visit them,
Last week they invited me;
That is how I can tell you
They live by a fòrlorn sea.

(They said: Here's a magic carpet,
Come on this,
And when you arrive
We will give you a big kiss.)

I play in the palace garden,
I climb the sycamore tree,
Sometimes I swim
In the fòrlorn sea.

The King and the Princess are shadowy,
Yet beautiful,
They are waited on by white cats,
Who are dutiful.

It is like a dream
When they kiss and cuddle me,
But I like it, I like it,
I do not wish to break free.

So I eat all they give me
Because I have read
If you eat fairy food
You will never wake up in your own bed,

But will go on living,
As has happened to me,
Far, far away
By a fòrlorn sea.

Angel Boley

THERE was a wicked woman called Malady Festing
Who lived with her son-in-law, Hark Boley,
And her daughter Angel,
In a house on the high moorlands
Of the West Riding of Yorkshire
In the middle of the last century.

One day Angel
Overheard her mother, Malady, talking to Hark, her
    husband.
Hark, said Malady, it is time
To take another couple of children
Into our kitchen.
Hark laughed, for he too was wicked and he knew
For what purpose the little children
Were required.

But Angel, who was not happy and so
Lived out her life in a dream of absentmindedness,
In order not to be too much aware
Of her horrible relatives, and what it was
That happened every now and then
In the kitchen; and why the children who came
Were never seen again, this time
When she heard what her husband and mother said,
Came out of her absentmindedness and paid attention.
I know now, she said, and all the time I have known
What I did not want to know, that they kill all children
They lure to this house; and that is why, when I pass in the
    village,
The people look askance at me, and they whisper—
But not so that I cannot hear—

There goes the daughter of Mother Lure. And the stranger
    says:
Who is Mother Lure? And they answer: Mrs Festing and
    they make the sign
That is to protect them from evil. Selfish wretches, said
    Angel,
They do not mind about the children, that evil is not kept
    from *them*.
Angel wandered into the woods and she said: No more
    children
Are going to be murdered, and before they are murdered,
    tormented
And corrupted; no more children are going to be the victims
Of Mother Lure and my husband, Hark. Dark was the
    look then
On Angel's face, and she said: I am the Angel of Death.

Mrs Festing and Boley
Always left the cooking to Angel, they despised Angel but
    Angel
Could cook, and that they thought was all she was fit for,
To cook and keep house. And they realised
It was far from being to their disadvantage that Angel was,
As they thought, half-witted, and never knew
Or wanted to know, what was going on around her.

As soon as Angel
Said to herself: I am the Angel of Death
She became at once very practical and went out into the
    woods and fields
And gathered some A. Phalloides, commonly called the
    'white' or deadly
Amanita, a mushroom of high toxicity. These poisonous fungi
She put into a soup, and this soup she gave
To Hark, and her mother, Malady, for supper, so that they
    died.

Angel then went to the police and said:
I have done evil, but I have saved many children.

The Judge said: Why did you not tell the police
That children were being destroyed? There was no proof,
    said Angel,
Because there were no bodies. I never could find out
What they did with the children after they had killed them.

So then the police searched hard, the wells, the rivers and
    the woodlands,
But never could they find out where
The children lay. Nor had the parents of the children
At any time done anything but weep. For they thought their
    children

Had been bewitched and done away with, and that
If they told their fears of Mother Lure and her wickedness
To the police, they would not believe them, and more
        children than ever
Would disappear.

From then onwards in the trial, Angel spoke
No word more, except to say: I am the Angel of Death.
So they put her in a lunatic asylum, and soon she died
Of an outbreak of typhoid fever. The people of the village
Now loved Angel, because she had delivered them from the fear

Of Mother Lure and Hark Boley, and had saved their
Little children from being tormented and slain by these
        wicked people.
So they wrote on her tombstone: 'She did evil that good
Might come'. But the Vicar said it was better not to put this but
Just her name and age, which was sixteen.
So he had the words
The villagers had written taken off the tombstone. But the
        next day
The words were again on the tombstone; so again the
        Vicar had them
Removed. And this time a watch was set on the grave,
A police constable and the village sexton watched there that night.

And no man came again to write on the tombstone
The forbidden words. Yet when morning came,
Again the words were on the tombstone.
So the Vicar said: It is the hand of the Lord.

And now in that graveyard, at that grave's head beneath
        the yew trees,
Still stands today the tombstone of Angel, with the
        words writ on it:
'She did evil that good might come'. May God be merciful.

Farewell

FAREWELL, dear friends,
I loved you so much,
But now I must leave you
And spread over me the dust.

Fair life fare well,
Fare never ill,
Far I go now
And say, Farewell.

Farewell, dear world,
With the waters around you curled
And the grass on your breast,
I loved you best.

Farewell fish and insect,
Bird, animal, swift mover,
Grim reptile as well,
I was your approver,

Wide sky, farewell,
Sun, moon, stars in places,
Farewell all fair universes
In far places.

Ding dong, ding dong,
As a bell is rung,
Sing ding dong farewell,
As a sweet bell.

The Donkey

I T was such a pretty little donkey
It had such pretty ears
And it used to gallop round the field so briskly
Though well down in years.

It was a retired donkey,
After a life-time of working
Between the shafts of regular employment
It was now free to go merrymaking.

Oh in its eyes was such a gleam
As is usually associated with youth
But it was not a youthful gleam really,
But full of mature truth.

And of the hilarity that goes with age,
As if to tell us sardonically
No hedged track lay before this donkey longer
But the sweet prairies of anarchy.

But the sweet prairies of anarchy
And the thought that keeps my heart up
That at last, in Death's odder anarchy,
Our pattern will be broken all up.
Though precious we are momentarily, donkey,
I aspire to be broken up.

Cock-a-Doo

I LOVE to hear the cock crow in
The middle of the day
It is an eerie sound in
The middle of the day
Sometimes it is a very hot day
Heavy for coming thunder
And the grass I tread on is dusty
And burnt yellow. Away
Over the river Bean which naturally
(It having been hot now for so long)
Runs shallow, stand up
The great yellow cornfields, but
Walking closely by the farm track
Not lifting my head, but foot by
Foot slowly, tired after a long
Walk, I see only the blue
And gray of the flint path, and
Each one of the particles of
Yellow dust on it. And this
Seeing, because of tiredness, becomes
A transfixion of seeing, more sharp
Than mirages are. Now comes the cry
Of the cock at midday
An eerie sound—cock-a-doooo—it
Sharpens a second time
The transfixion. If there were
A third sharpener
Coming this hot day with a butcher's edge
It would spell death.

Francesca in Winter

O LOVE sweet love
I feel this love
It burns me so
It comes not from above

It burns me so
The flames run close
Can you not see
How the flames toss

Our souls like paper
On the air?
Our souls are white
As ashes are

O love sweet love
Will our love burn
Love till our love
To ashes turn?

I wish hellfire
Played fire's part
And burnt to end
Flesh soul and heart

Then we could sit beside our fire
With quiet love
Not fear to look in flames and see
A shadow move.

Ah me, only
In heaven's permission
Are creatures quiet
In their condition.

26

So to fatness come

Poor human race that must
Feed on pain, or choose another dish
And hunger worse.

There is also a cup of pain, for
You to drink all up, or,
Setting it aside for sweeter drink,
Thirst evermore.

I am thy friend. I wish
You to sup full of the dish
I give you and the drink,
And so to fatness come more than you think
In health of opened heart, and know peace.

Grief spake these words to me in a dream. I thought
He spoke no more than grace allowed
And no less than truth.

The Sallow Bird

A sallow bird sat on a tree
Yclad in black from head to hee'
And oh he wept sae piteously.

Why sitst thou there and a' so blackit?
Why sitst thou there in thy black jacket,
With feathers furled?

Ah me, ah me,
Come now, tell me.

Then spake the bird in accents sar'
    'Something human's dearer far
    To me than wealth of a' the world,
    And I lack it, and I lack it, I lack it.'

Never seyd he word again
(Nor went away). Yet oft in pain
He'll hauk that crik as if he spak it:
'I lack it, I lack it, I lack it.'

When Walking

A TALENTED old gentleman painting a hedge
Came suddenly upon my mind's eye when walking;
Forgive me for my sins
And bring me to everlasting life to be with
    thee in happiness for ever,
I wanted to say. But I could not.
My heart leaps, I said. I am filled with joy
For your hedge. Nodding, he vanishèd.

Her-zie

*(A troll and his wife speak of the human
child they stole.)*

WHAT's wrong with you-zie?
Nothing with me-zie,
Then what with who-zie?
Only with Her-zie,
So what with Her-zie?
A hearse for her-zie
A hearse for her-zie
Came for her.

What colour was it then?
Golden, golden,
Was there anyone in it?
A pale king was in it.
That was not a hearse for Her-zie, husband,
It was her marriage carriage.
It was a hearse for me, then,
My heart went with them and died then.

Husband, ah me-zie,
Your heart has died for Her-zie,
Without it you cannot be easy.

The Word

My heart leaps up with streams of joy,
My lips tell of drouth;
Why should my heart be full of joy
And not my mouth?

I fear the Word, to speak or write it down,
I fear all that is brought to birth and born;
This fear has turned my joy into a frown.

Nor *We of Her to Him*

HE said no word of her to us
Nor we of her to him,
But oh it saddened us to see
How wan he grew and thin.
We said: She eats him day and night
And draws the blood from him,
We did not know but said we thought
This was why he grew thin.

One day we called and rang the bell,
No answer came within,
We said: She must have took him off
To the forest old and grim,
It has fell out, we said, that she
Eats him in forest grim,
And how can we help him being eaten
Up in forests grim?

It is a restless time we spend,
We have no help for him,
We walk about and go to bed,
It is no help to him.
Sometimes we shake our heads and say
It might have better been
If he had spoke to us of her
Or we of her to him.
Which makes us feel helpful, until
The silence comes again.

Mrs Blow and Her Animals

THERE was a dog called Clanworthy
Who lived with his friend the cat Hopdance
In the house of Mrs Blow, a widow,
Upon a glade in Cluny.

Hey, Hopdance,
How is Mrs Blow?
So-so, said Hopdance,
Bow, said the dog.

Mrs Blow
Loved her animals very much
She often said:
I do not know what I should do
Without Hopdance and
Clanworthy.

They loved her too.

Hey, Hopdance,
How is Mrs Blow?
So-so, said Hopdance,
She is not very well, said the dog.

Hopdance fetched her a fish
Which she cooked by the fire.
That will do her good,
Said Hopdance; but, said the dog,
She must have wine as well as food.

Clanworthy, brave Clanworthy,
Clanworthy for aye
Through fire and water brought wine
That Mrs Blow might not die.

Mrs Blow has now become their only thought
And care,
All the other animals

In the forest of Cluny
Say there is no talking to them now
Because their only thought is Mrs Blow.

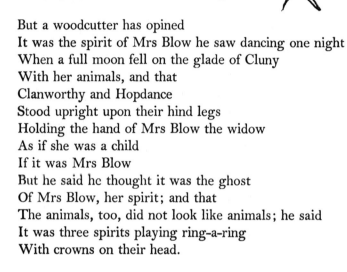

Hey, Hopdance,
How is Mrs Blow?
Oh, very well now.
She is quite recovered, said the dog.

But a woodcutter has opined
It was the spirit of Mrs Blow he saw dancing one night
When a full moon fell on the glade of Cluny
With her animals, and that
Clanworthy and Hopdance
Stood upright upon their hind legs
Holding the hand of Mrs Blow the widow
As if she was a child
If it was Mrs Blow
But he said he thought it was the ghost
Of Mrs Blow, her spirit; and that
The animals, too, did not look like animals; he said
It was three spirits playing ring-a-ring
With crowns on their head.

So everyone remembered then
That a long time ago
The King and Queen had lost their little children
As
A great witch had changed the boys into animals
And the girl into Mrs Blow the widow

Crying: Hopdance, go Hopdance; Clanworthy go,
For a hundred and seven years
Be the animals of Mrs Blow.

Everyone was glad it had come right
And that the princes and the princess
Were dancing in the night.

Oh grateful colours, bright looks!

THE grass is green
The tulip is red
A ginger cat walks over
The pink almond petals on the flower bed.
Enough has been said to show
It is life we are talking about. Oh
Grateful colours, bright looks! Well, to go
On. Fabricated things too—front doors and gates,
Bricks, slates, paving stones—are coloured
And as it has been raining and is sunny now
They shine. Only that puddle
Which, reflecting the height of the sky
Quite gives one a feeling of vertigo, shows
No colour, is a negative. Men!
Seize colours quick, heap them up while you can.
But perhaps it is a false tale that says
The landscape of the dead
Is colourless.

O Pug!

(*To the Brownes' pug dog, on my lap, in their car,
coming home from Norfolk.*)

O Pug, some people do not like you,
But I like you,
Some people say you do not breathe, you snore,
I don't mind,
One person says he is always conscious of your behind,
Is that your fault?

Your own people love you,
All the people in the family that owns you
Love you: Good pug, they cry, Happy pug,
Pug-come-for-a-walk.

You are an old dog now
And in all your life
You have never had cause for a moment's anxiety,
Yet,
In those great eyes of yours,
Those liquid and protuberant orbs,
Lies the shadow of immense insecurity. There
Panic walks.

Yes, yes, I know,
When your mistress is with you,
When your master
Takes you upon his lap,
Just then, for a moment,
Almost you are not frightened.

But at heart you are frightened, you always have been.

O Pug, obstinate old nervous breakdown,
In the midst of *so* much love,
And such comfort,
Still to feel unsafe and be afraid,

How one's heart goes out to you!

Archie and Tina

ARCHIE and Tina
Where are you now,
Playmates of my childhood,
Brother and sister?

When we stayed in the same place
With Archie and Tina
At the seaside,
We used

To paddle the samphire beds, fish
Crabs from the sea-pool, poke
The anemones, run,
Trailing the ribbon seaweed across the sand to the sea's edge
To throw it in as far out as we could. We dug
White bones of dead animals from the sandhills, found
The jaw-bone of a fox with some teeth in it, a stoat's skull,
The hind leg of a hare.

Oh, if only; oh if only!

Archie and Tina
Had a dog called Bam. The silver-sand
Got in his long hair. He had
To be taken home.

Oh, if only . . . !

One day when the wind blew strong
Our dog, Boy, got earache. He had
To be taken home in a jersey.

Oh what pleasure, what pleasure!

There never were so many puppies as there were then,
So much yellow corn, so many fine days,
Such sharp bright air, such seas.

Was it necessary that
Archie and Tina, Bam and Boy,
Should have been there too?
Yes, then it was. But to say now:

Where are you today
Archie and Tina,
Playmates of my childhood,
Brother and sister? Is no more than to say:

I remember
Such pleasure, so much pleasure.

The Poet Hin

THE foolish poet wonders
Why so much honour
Is given to other poets
But to him
No honour is given.

I am much condescended to, said the poet Hin,
By my inferiors. And, said the poet Hin,
On my tombstone I will have inscribed:
'He was much condescended to by his inferiors.'
Then, said the poet Hin,
I shall be properly remembered.

Hin—wiping his tears away, I cried—
Your words tell me
You know the correct use of *shall* and *will*.
That, Hin, is something we may think about,
May, may, may, man.

Well yes, true, said Hin, stopping crying then,
Well yes, but true only in part,
Well, your wiping my tears away
Was a part.

But ah me, ah me,
So much vanity, said he, is in my heart.
Yet not light always is the pain
That roots in levity. Or without fruit wholly
As from this levity's
Flowering pang of melancholy
May grow what is weighty,
May come beauty.

True too, Hin, true too. Well, as now: You have gone on
Differently from what you begun.
Yet both truths have validity,
The one meanly begot, the other nobly,
And as each alone glosses over
What the other says, so only together
Have they a full thought to uncover.

The House of Over-Dew

OVER-DEW
Became a dread name for Cynthia
In 1937
It was then that Mr Minnim first began to talk openly
About his dear wish.
How dear it was to be
For all of them!

Mr and Mrs Minnim had two sons
Who had done well at school
And won scholarships to Oxford.
Their boyhood was a happy time for all. Then
The elder son married Helen,
A fellow-student at the university,
And, coming down, found a good post with sufficient money.
His wife also
Had money of her own, they were doing well.

The younger son, Georgie,
Was engaged to Cynthia. But that did not go so well.
He took a First in Greats, but then
The difficulties began. He could not find a job.
He did nothing, tried again; no good.
He grew sulky. It seemed hopeless.

It was now that the dread name of Over-Dew
Was spoken,
And a scheme bruited. It was this:
The Minnims were sincere and practising Christians, to
      Mr Minnim
Anyone who was not a Christian
Was a half-educated person.
It was, for instance, suggested
That his daughter-in-law should write a Life of St Benedict,
There was no good life of St Benedict, said Mr Minnim.
So Cynthia suggested that Helen should write it,
Because Helen was a Mediaeval History student,

Whereas Cynthia herself was a Latinist,
So why not Helen, with her special knowledge?
But Helen was not a Christian,
So, 'No', said Mr Minnim, she was a half-educated person.

The Over-Dew scheme was orthodox Christian.
When Mr Minnim retired from his accountancy work
He said that they should move from the suburb where
    they lived
And buy the house of Over-Dew, which was
A retreat for missionaries to have
On their leave-holidays in England.
And now it was being run, he said, in a fantastical fashion.

When they bought it
Everything would be better,
And different.
Where was the money to come from? No matter,
They had their savings, also they had the faith
Of Mr and Mrs Minnim.

Mrs Minnim loved her husband
And was pleased to follow him to the end of the earth,
    and certainly
Over-Dew was not that.

But oh when Cynthia heard that word
It was the knell
Of all her life and love. This, she said,
Is the end of happy days and the beginning
Of calamity. Over-Dew, she thought,
Shall be the death of my love and the death of life.
For to that time, she thought,
Shall come up a European war and personal defeat.

The Georgie situation
Was already sad. What could she do there?
                                        Nothing,
But see him and be silent and so enrage,
Or see him and speak, and the more enrage.

The wise and affectionate Cynthia
Must break the engagement and give back the ring.
There is nothing but this that she can do.
She takes up a post at London University
And in lecturing and study passes the days.
No more of that.

She has read a paper to her pupils
And fellow-dons, the subject is
The development of Latin from the first early growth
Upon the Grecian models. The study entrances,
She finds and reads a Latin prayer:
'I devote to Hades and Destruction'. It is a prayer
For time of battle, the thought is this:
I dedicate the enemy to Hades and Destruction.
                                        And perhaps

One or two of the praying Romans
Will devote also themselves
To Hades and Destruction. Rushing then into battle,
These 'devoted' people hope they may be killed.
                                                    If not,
They are held for dead,
They are stateless, and in religion
Have no part at all. The gods have not accepted them,
They are alive, but yet they are destroyed.

In Cynthia's life, this sad year
Was twice as long as all the happy years before.
                                          She must now
Withdraw from Georgie and see him miserable.

She is at work and fast within her family,
The happy careless laughter
Of the brothers and sisters
Rings her round,
She has the home tasks, too,
And thinks of Georgie.

At the end of the year, in the bitter snow that fell that
        Christmas
The phrenzied Minnims
Moved from their life-long suburb.

The house of Over-Dew
Lay buried half in snow,
It stood five miles from any town upon a hillside.
Very bleak it was, and all the pipes were froze.
Mrs Minnim worked hard,
They had a girl to help them then she left.

Mrs Minnim had courage and was cheerful
But she was by now an old lady. Suddenly
There was the gift of a little money. Mr Minnim
Bought chasubles for visiting priests. But at first
There were no visitors at all, but only
The old cold house, and the lavatories frozen up
And wood kindling to be chopped and dried.
The work was bitter hard.
Mr Minnim, released suddenly
From the routine of his accountancy
Suffered in his head a strange numbness,
He moved about in a dream, would take no hand with the
        dishes. Even
When five-and-twenty missionaries came for a conference
He would do nothing.
He paced the garden plots, 'And here' he said,
'I will build twelve lavatories. And in this room
We will have a consecration and build an altar.'

The thaw came and turned all to mud and slush,
There was still no post for Georgie, he came down from
        Oxford
And washed the dishes for his mother,
And chopped the wood and moved also in a daze,
The immense learning
Lay off from him, the crude work of the house
Was an excuse from study.

But now Mrs Minnim was not happy, like a sad animal
She roamed the rooms of Over-Dew. This woman
Who had been so boisterous and so loving
With many friends, but still her own best thoughts
For Mr Minnim and their sons,
Was like a sad animal that cannot know a reason.

Georgie, with the guilt of the excuse upon his heart,
Grew savage with her. The moody silences
Were shot with cruel words
It was so bitter cold within the house
Though now without the snow was melted and turned to
    slush.

The money situation preyed upon the mind of Mrs Minnim.

But her husband
Spoke of faith.

In the suburb where they once lived friends said:
How are the Minnims? Did you hear
That Mr Minnim had bought chasubles?
And then the foolish, unkind laughter: Chasubles!
It will be
The ruin of them, the end.

There was one hope that Mrs Minnim had, it was this,
That they might return at last to their house in the suburb,
She had refused to let her husband
Sell this house. No, that she would not allow, No,
That must be for a return.
But now, out of this refusal was made
The bitterness of their life at Over-Dew. For, said her
    husband,
You kept back the seven hundred and fifty pounds
We might have had for selling the house.

In London
The girl who should have been Georgie's wife
Hears all; understands; loves Georgie; is helpless;
                        reads to her class
The Latin prayer: I devote to Hades and Destruction.
She rules the harsh thoughts that run; cries;
'Come, love of God.'

Oblivion

It was a human face in my oblivion
A human being and a human voice
That cried to me, Come back, come back, come back.
But I would not, I said I would not come back.

It was so sweet in my oblivion
There was a sweet mist wrapped me round about
And I trod in a sweet and milky sea, knee deep,
That was so pretty and so beautiful, growing deeper.

But still the voice cried out, Come back, come back,
Come back to me from sweet oblivion!
It was a human and related voice
That cried to me in pain. So I turned back.

I cannot help but like Oblivion better
Than being a human heart and human creature,
But I can wait for her, her gentle mist
And those sweet seas that deepen are my destiny
And must come even if not soon.

The Galloping Cat

Oh I am a cat that likes to
Gallop about doing good
So
One day when I was
Galloping about doing good, I saw
A Figure in the path; I said:
Get off! (Be-
cause
I am a cat that likes to
Gallop about doing good)
But he did not move, instead
He raised his hand as if
To land me a cuff
So I made to dodge so as to
Prevent him bringing it orf,
Un-for-tune-ately I slid
On a banana skin
Some Ass had left instead
Of putting in the bin. So
His hand caught me on the cheek
I tried
To lay his arm open from wrist to elbow
With my sharp teeth
Because I am
A cat that likes to gallop about doing good.
Would you believe it?
He wasn't there
My teeth met nothing but air,
But a Voice said: Poor cat,
(Meaning me) and a soft stroke
Came on me head
Since when
I have been bald.

I regard myself as
A martyr to doing good.
Also I heard a swoosh
As of wings, and saw
A halo shining at the height of
Mrs Gubbins's backyard fence,
So I thought: What's the good
Of galloping about doing good
When angels stand in the path
And do not do as they should
Such as having an arm to be bitten off
All the same I
Intend to go on being
A cat that likes to
Gallop about doing good
So
Now with my bald head I go,
Chopping the untidy flowers down, to
                              and fro,
An' scooping up the grass to show
Underneath
The cinder path of wrath
Ha ha ha ha, ho,
Angels aren't the only ones who do
                              not know
What's what and that
Galloping about doing good
Is a full-time job
That needs
An experienced eye of earthly
Sharpness, worth I dare say
(If you'll forgive a personal note)
A good deal more
Than all that skyey stuff
Of angels that make so bold as
To pity a cat like me that
Gallops about doing good.

Hippy-Mo

I HAD a sweet bird
Called Hippy-Mo
But he did not wish to stay
With me, he wished to go.
Hippy-Mo, Hippy-Mo.

I hugged him tight, I said:
You shall not go,
You shall stay here with me
Hippy-Mo.

Then he grew tall as a house,
Hippy-Mo,
Took me in his claws and would
Not let me go,
Hippy-Mo.

His eyes were black as the night
Through which we flew,
And the lightnings flashed from his eyes
As we flew through,
Hippy-Mo what are
You going to do
With me?

Hippy-Mo, Hippy-Mo,
Brought me to a sunny land.
Put me in a cage
Wherein I rage
And when I rage he holds
My hand
So tight I cannot move
From him.

Hippy-Mo
Let me go,
Do you wish me
To die?

He was so mean he did not condescend
To reply. Even
Yes or no.

Hendecasyllables

It is the very bewitching hour of eight
Which is the moment when my new day begins,
I love to hear the pretty clock striking eight
I love to get up out of my bed quickly.
Why is this? Because morning air is so cold?
Or because of new strength that seems to come then?
Both. And also because waking up ends dreams.

Black March

I HAVE a friend
At the end
Of the world.
His name is a breath

Of fresh air.
He is dressed in
Grey chiffon. At least
I think it is chiffon.
It has a
Peculiar look, like smoke.

It wraps him round
It blows out of place
It conceals him
I have not seen his face.

But I have seen his eyes, they are
As pretty and bright
As raindrops on black twigs
In March, and heard him say:

I am a breath
Of fresh air for you, a change
By and by.

Black March I call him
Because of his eyes
Being like March raindrops
On black twigs.

(Such a pretty time when the sky
Behind black twigs can be seen
Stretched out in one
Uninterrupted
Cambridge blue as cold as snow.)

But this friend
Whatever new names I give him
Is an old friend. He says:

Whatever names you give me
I am
A breath of fresh air,
A change for you.

Grave by a Holm-Oak

You lie there, Anna,
In your grave now,
Under a snow-sky,
You lie there now.

Where have the dead gone?
Where do they live now?
Not in the grave, they say,
Then where now?

Tell me, tell me,
Is it where I may go?
Ask not, cries the holm-oak,
Weep, says snow.

The Sea-widow

How fares it with you, Mrs Cooper my bride?
Long are the years since you lay by my side.
Do you wish I was back? Do you speak of me dearest?
I wish you were back for me to hold nearest.
Who then lies nearer, Mrs Cooper my bride?
A black man comes in with the evening tide.
What is his name? Tell me! How does he dare?
He comes uninvited. His name is Despair.

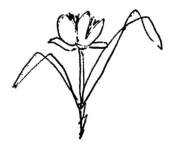

The Stroke
(For M)

I was a beautiful plant
I stood in the garden supreme
Till there came a blight that fell on each leaf
How I wish this had not been
Oh I wish this had not been.

I can feel the sun, and my blighted leaves
In an elderly way grow glad
But oh in my depths I bleed, I bleed,
From a heart that is youthful and sad
From a heart that is piercèd and sad.

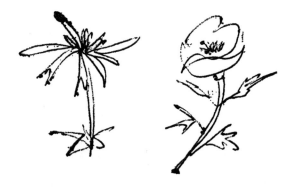

Come, Death

I FEEL ill. What can the matter be?
I'd ask God to have pity on me,
But I turn to the one I know, and say:
Come, Death, and carry me away.

Ah me, sweet Death, you are the only god
Who comes as a servant when he is called, you know,
Listen then to this sound I make, it is sharp,
Come Death. Do not be slow.